The Gospel of the Kingdom
for
Kids, Tweens, and Teens

by Lauren Caldwell

Thank you Dr. Henry Malone for writing Shadow Boxing©. FMI www.visionlife.org

Collaborator/Editor Kevin McSpadden
Illustrated by Matthew Butcher
Format and Design by Grant Hill

Requests for information should be addressed to:
Garden Publishing Company LLC.
Email:info@gardenpublishingcompany.com
Web site: http://www.gardenpublishingcompany.com

ISBN 978-0-9833377-0-6
Printed in the United States of America.

About the Author

Lauren Caldwell lives on a ranch in West Texas. She enjoys spending time with her husband, Cliff, and their three children. Lauren serves in leadership at The Garden Apostolic Training Center in San Angelo, Texas. "The Garden" hosts a school of ministry for adults and children to train the saints to minister to the poor and homeless, young mothers, hurting women, and just about any facet of life the Kingdom of Heaven touches.

The Garden ministers to people from all over the world and would love to help you in any way it can. Please contact the Garden through the website Http://www.thegardenstc.org or email Lauren directly at lauren@thegardenstc.org

Introduction

In the January of 2006 my life was forever changed. My eyes were opened to the rest of a story I'd only partially known. The small part of the story I knew was the foundation of my life, so imagine how surpised I was to find out there was so much more to it.

You see, I had known Jesus from an early age. I thought I knew all it meant to be saved. I had been in church all my life. I loved Jesus and Father God with all my heart. I respected the Holy Spirit. I even lead people to Jesus and taught Sunday School.

What I didn't know was that there was much more to this journey of faith than I had ever imagined. There was more to being a Christian than I had known. The "more" is what I share in this book. This is actually an expanded version of the first chapter of another book, There's No Junior Holy Spirit: A Supernatural Training Manual for Youth. This is a stand alone version because it is a foundation or the beginning of the rest of the story. If you get this part, the other parts of the story make more sense.

Read on, and enjoy the beginning of the rest of the story...

First things first – what does it even mean to be "saved" or have "salvation?" Here's what I knew growing up: it meant to give your life to Jesus or invite Him into your heart. I didn't have to go to Hell, and I was forgiven for all of the bad stuff I ever did. Not bad, huh? But wait, there's more!

Now you would think if I spent my whole life going to church and reading the Bible, I might look up "salvation" in the dictionary or something. I mean really, if this was for a test in school, it would be a vocabulary word and a no-brainer as a test question! So what is the definition of the word?

When we look up Bible words, we go back to the Greek and Hebrew languages for definitions because those are the languages in which the Bible was written back then. The words still mean the same thing in English, but the older languages sometimes have extra ideas hidden inside them too. It is important to get to the nitty-gritty of the words we look up.

All that to say, if you look up "salvation" in the Greek language, it means:

Sozo /Soteria – Eternal life, forgiveness of sins, healing, rescued from evil, protection, wholeness, and prosperity (to move forward in every area of your life).

So, not only do we get to go to Heaven when we die and get forgiven for all we've ever done wrong, but we also get healed, get rescued from evil, and get to move forward in all areas of our life. We are protected by God as well, and we don't have to have anything missing or broken. Many times in the Bible, the word "saved" could be translated "healed, delivered, etc." Excellent deal, huh? Here are a few questions though...

Saved from what? Why didn't we just get born this way? Did Jesus really have to die to get something back for us, and if so, how did we lose it in the first place?

Here's a basic version of what happened:

Father, Son, and Holy Spirit have always existed and will always exist. A common question I hear is, "So where did God come from?" Honestly, I don't know. I do know that He exists because the Bible says He does, I see evidence of Him in creation, and I have actually encountered Him in my life. There are people who thrive on a part of Christianity called "Apologetics," (the study and defense of our beliefs) and I encourage you to find out more about Apologetics so you can find specific answers. It would take more writing on that specific topic to explain it, so seek it out yourself.

To continue: Father, Son, and Holy Spirit have always existed. They are perfect in every way. They chose to create a planet with living things on it. I have the idea that they wanted to spread their love, so they agreed together to create a planet and furnish it for their children. The first family was a perfect creation in the image of God. Father, Son, and Holy Spirit delighted in perfect relationship with Adam and Eve.

Some point before time on earth began, Lucifer, whose name means "light bringer," was one of God's angels. The Bible says he used to be beautiful, and his whole body was designed to worship God. Because he thought so much of himself, Lucifer decided he would be the king of heaven and rule it instead of God. One third of the angels joined Lucifer and waged war against God for control of everything. Of course they lost and got thrown out of Heaven by God. We aren't sure exactly when this happened, but we know that it did.

Meanwhile, around this time Father God had created the earth. He breathed life into Adam and created Eve. He put them in a beautiful garden called Eden, and their job was to rule over everything and spread out God's garden across the whole earth. Father God basically gave Adam and Eve the keys to the earth and said, "Let's be a family and take care of this together." I know you are excited about getting keys to a car someday. Can you imagine having the keys to the whole planet?

For a while, Father God and his children enjoyed perfect friendship. God even walked around on earth with them and taught them things Himself. They saw Him with their eyes and were His "BFF's!" They knew what made each other laugh. Father loved watching them learn about and enjoy what He had given them, and Adam and Eve loved their Daddy. It was actually the perfect family.

As you well know, every family has rules. This family only had two rules. The first was to be totally obedient to God as they spread the garden, which was a lot like Heaven, over the whole earth. The second was that Adam and Eve were not supposed to eat the fruit of one particular tree because it would kill them if they did. Easy enough, right?

Let's enjoy each other and spread this love over the whole world... just don't eat of this one tree, you'll die.
-Genesis 2:17

Well, Lucifer (now called Satan, the accuser) hated God for booting him out of Heaven and giving the keys to a mere human. Satan knew he couldn't whip God, so he went for the next best thing – God's family.

Have you ever seen someone rip up a picture or scribble on a picture of someone? It really hurts a person's feelings when someone does that to them. So that's what Satan started doing to God. You see, we are made in God's image. We're like a picture of our Father. Satan tries to rip us up or scribble on our lives because he is no match for the real thing, our maker, Father God. Instead, he picks on us to get to Him.

Remember, Daddy God gave his kiddos the keys to the planet, and Satan lost the battle to rule Heaven. Adam and Eve were supposed to make something like a copy of Heaven on Earth. Satan wanted Heaven, but would settle for the copy. You have to realize that God and Satan aren't equals, so there was no way for Satan to compete with God's power. That's why Satan had to come up with a scheme to gain control of the earth.

Satan knew if he could get Adam and Eve on his side, he could take control of what their Father had given them. It was like a movie where the bitter person tries to steal the family land from those who rightfully own it. Satan fooled Eve. He told her she could be like God and know about good and evil if she only ate fruit from the one tree on the planet Father God said was off limits. Have you ever wanted to do something just because someone told you not to? You've got great-great-grandma Eve to thank for falling on that one.

Well, she listened to Satan and ate the fruit. The sad part of the story is that Adam, who was right beside Eve the whole time, also ate the forbidden fruit. Argh! You may be wondering, "Why'd they have to be such suckers?!" Honestly, they were the perfect examples of what you and I would do, so get over it. But here's where we get into some of the things I didn't know.

Remember, God had told Adam that if he ate of the fruit he would die. Yet, when they both ate it they didn't croak. Say what? Is God a liar? Nope. I'll bet this next part is going to help a few things make more sense for you. It did for me.

God is a three part being in a way. (Don't even ask me to explain how Father God, Jesus, and Holy Spirit are all God, yet somehow separate. They just are. All three are equally God. Yes, even Holy Spirit.) So we are made in three parts, too, according to the Bible. We have a BODY. We have a SOUL. We have a SPIRIT.

"Now may the God of peace Himself sanctify you completely, and may your whole spirit and soul and body be kept blameless at the coming of our Lord Jesus Christ. He who calls you is faithful; He will surely do it." 1 Thessalonians 5:23-24 ESV

So, how exactly does this work for you? Well first, you have a body, which is made of all the parts of you that you can see and touch. Your soul is your mind, will, and emotions. In other words, your soul is how you think, act, and feel. And your spirit is where your connection with God is.

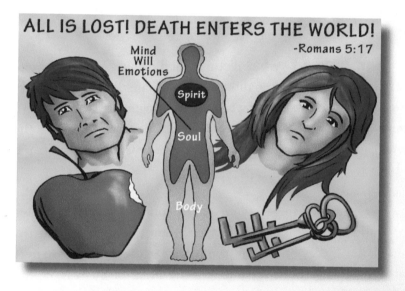

So what happened to Adam? The best I can explain is that when Adam believed Satan over God and ate the fruit, his spirit died. I always picture it as just going out like a flame. Suddenly, Adam no longer had his connection to Father. That's the bad news. The good news is that Jesus, as the son of God, agreed ahead of time that He would be the hero to come and rescue humanity if they ever needed it. You'll see how that fits soon.

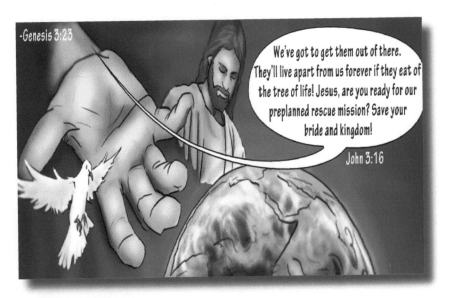

For a long time, I pictured God being really hacked off because of what His children did. I imagined Him kind of turning His back on Adam and Eve and maybe even pouting a bit. Now, I see it so differently. They were God's best friends on the whole earth, yet they believed His enemy more than Him. Wow, poor God's heart. He must have been so sad.

Now God had to get Adam and Eve out of the garden because there was this other tree we don't always think about. It was the tree of eternal life. If they had eaten from that tree they would have lived on earth forever and been separated from Father for the rest of eternity. So He had to get them out and put an intense angel at the gate to keep them from getting back in and getting fooled into eating from that tree, too.

But God knew what to do to make things right, and He already had a plan. Remember, before it all began, Jesus had agreed to make things right for us and be our hero if we needed one. Now, we really needed a hero. So God set his plan in motion and started getting things ready for Jesus to come to our rescue.

Time out here.

Just so you know, there are some things for which I don't exactly have the answer. Instead of telling you what I think or what I've heard or read, I'm just going to leave it up to you to find out. Maybe you can help me out! For example, you might ask why God didn't zap Lucifer into a Cheeto® and get on with it. I don't know the answer for certain, so I'll let you wrestle that out for yourself.

Prophets... Daniel Joseph, Moses, David Elijah, Hosea, Ezekiel Solomon, Elisha, John the Baptist

Through this time, many told of Jesus's rescue mission and partnered with God to prepare the world to be His bride and welcome the Good Kingdom of God & light & heaven VS. The Bad Kingdom of EVIL & DARKNESS. Then it was finally time for the kindom to come and bride to live...

After a perfect amount of time, Father God worked out His plan. The advertising campaign, also known as prophecies, had been going on for hundreds of years. All the prophets told of a great hero who could come to rescue the world. When the time came, Jesus was born.

Since spiritual death is passed on from parents to their children, Jesus had to have Holy Spirit as His Father. Otherwise he would have inherited His great, great, great, grandfather Adam's dead spirit. And you thought you just got your dad's nose or eyes when you were born! Nope, that spiritual death was passed right on through our ancestors and is still going on with everyone born today. That's why when you were born, guess what? You were not born innocent. Even David from the Bible knew that.

Have you ever seen anyone teach a toddler to be selfish? Nope, we start out with that "instinct." So, that's why when you believe in Jesus and Holy Spirit comes to live inside you, it is called being born again! You are born again in your spirit. But I'm getting ahead of myself.

Jesus was born of the Holy Spirit and a human (Mary) to do what Adam was supposed to do. He's even called the second Adam in the Bible. Jesus was born with his connection to God intact, so He never fell for Satan's lies or temptations. He was the only one who could win the right to take the keys to the planet back from Satan. In order for that to happen, though, somebody had to pay for all the wrong done all the way back to Adam. Jesus had the right to pay for all those mistakes, including ours, because He didn't make any. He perfectly obeyed Father God. Jesus was so obedient that He even obeyed Death.

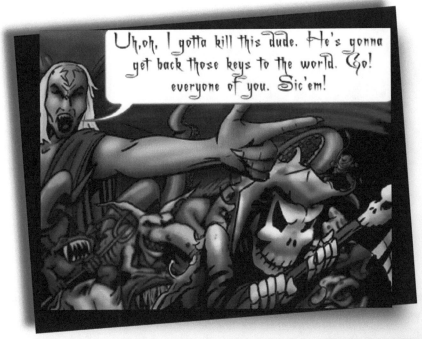

When Jesus obediently went to the cross carrying the entire world's brokenness, Death and Satan thought they'd beaten the second Adam, too. That is, they thought they had defeated Him until God let them know things were good with His family again because the price had been paid. God raised Jesus from the dead to show that all the wrongs were now completely paid for, and we could live again connected to our Father God, just like in the garden.

It is almost like Jesus hit an "overs" button for us all, and we're back to the original plan God had for humans. When we believe Father God loves us and sent His son to pay for our wrong-doings, we gain the advantage over Satan that Adam lost. It's not like God changed His mind about what He wanted to do with the planet! He still wants us to bring His kingdom to the earth. So when we're born again in the spirit, we get to do what Adam and Eve were supposed to do. Jesus got the keys and authority back and gave them to us. Jesus also gave us His Holy Spirit to live inside of us and empower us to do what He created us to do. We've just got to clean up a few messes Satan makes along the way.

"Whoever makes a practice of sinning is of the devil for the devil has been sinning from the beginning. The reason the Son of God appeared was to destroy the works of the devil." 1 John 3:8 ESV

Jesus was punished for our sakes. Satan's power was left nailed to the cross, not Jesus. He disarmed the enemy, made them look bad in public and triumphed over them. The keys and authority are His.
Colossians 2:14-15
Revelation 1:18
Isaiah 53

What's going on in there?

If you haven't come to the time in your life where Jesus Christ has not only saved you, but is your boss, you can do that right now. You can take Father up on His amazing rescue plan. Jesus is the only way to get back what was stolen – your rightful family. If you want to be rescued out of the Kingdom of Darkness and Hell and be born again into the Kingdom of Light and Heaven, today is your day. Pray this or something like it:

"Father , I admit I've done just what Adam and Eve did. I've chosen to listen to the enemy and chosen my own way instead of yours. I was born dead in my spirit and I want to be born again by your Holy Spirit. I want to give you my entire life. I will serve you and love you forever. Please rescue me, forgive me, heal me and bring me peace. I believe Jesus was your son and He died so I didn't have to. Please take care of me and love me forever. Thank you, and I want to have everything you have for me in Jesus' Name."

Now, if you just gave your life to Jesus, find someone else who knows Him and tell them. It is time for you to be taught how this new Kingdom works. Ask your Heavenly Father to help you find someone to grow you up into a mighty vicious warrior for His glory.

GOSPEL OF THE KINGDOM
vs.
GOSPEL OF SALVATION

What is the difference between the Gospel of the Kingdom and the Gospel of Salvation? Once again, let's get definitions of what we're talking about.

Gospel- something regarded as true and believed, good news
Kingdom- where a king or queen rules, a domain
Dominion- a land or territory where a king rules and has authority
Salvation- Sozo /Soteria - forgiveness of sins, eternal life, healing, rescued from evil, protection, wholeness, and provision(going forward in all areas of your life)

So when we talk about the Gospel of Salvation, we are talking about all of those things described under Salvation happening within us and for us. The Gospel of the Kingdom is basically extending what's happening within us to the territory around us. That's why in Matthew chapter 6 Jesus taught us to pray, "Your kingdom come, Your will be done, on earth as it is in Heaven." We bring one kingdom to take the place of another. We make a transfer from Earth's kingdom to Heaven's Kingdom.

My family lives on a ranch in West Texas. This ranch has been passed down or inherited in this family for five generations. Ranches have boundaries and gates. Entering the gates of the ranch is like receiving salvation. You get in and it is your inheritance. You are happy to be in and receive the benefits, but wouldn't it be silly if you only sat inside the gates? You would miss out on all the fun stuff there is to do and see in the ranch! Plus there's work to do on a ranch. There are things that need to be repaired, pests to run off, and improvements to make. Doing the work on the ranch and maintaining or extending the land are good examples of dominion and a kingdom. Father God is the owner and boss of the ranch and we are co-heirs with Jesus. We do what the Father says in partnership with Jesus. The Holy Spirit gives us instruction and power to take care of the ranch. Or the garden. Or the whole world.

Questions

1. Sozo/Soteria includes 1) _____ of sins 2) _____ life with God 3) healing for body and _____ 4) rescue from _____ 5)protection 6) wholeness 7) _____.

2. We are made of three parts: 1)_____ 2) _____3) spirit.

3. According to John 3:8 the reason the Son of God appeared was to_____.

4. The Gospel of Salvation is like _____ the gates of a ranch.

5. Doing the work or extending the ranch is like the Gospel of the _____.

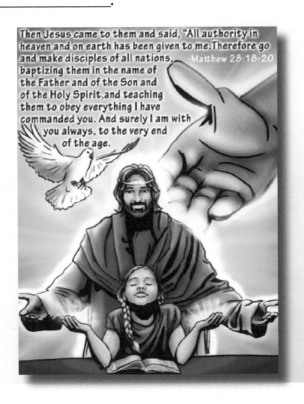

The Garden Apostolic Training Center is primarily a School of Ministry in San Angelo, Texas that fosters spiritual growth. The center provides training to equip believers in Jesus Christ for the work of the ministry and to be victorious in all areas of their lives through the supernatural empowerment of the Holy Spirit.

There are several ministries and companies that are partnered with The Garden or are a facet of the ministry. Below are the following ministries and companies.

 — The Garden School of Ministry is a two year school that prepares Christians to minister as Jesus did and does.

 -- Company 68 is a ministry under The Garden that desires to see wounded women empowered to fufill their destiny in God.

 --Providence is a ministry under The Garden targeting the poor and homeless men, women, and children in San Angelo's region.

 --Garden Publishing Company is company that publishes, edits, and formats works for publication.

 -- M-4 Initiative is The Garden school of ministry for eqipping kids in the love of God, intimacy with Jesus and power of the Holy Spirit.

Gospel of the Kingdom Answers:

Questions for Book

1. Sozo/Soteria includes 1) **forgiveness** of sins 2) **eternal** life with God 3) healing for body and **soul** 4) rescue from **evil** 5) protection 6) wholeness 7) **prosperity**.

2. We are made of three parts: **1) body 2) soul 3) spirit**.

3. According to John 3:8 the reason the Son of God appeared was to **destroy the works of the devil**.

4. The Gospel of Salvation is like **entering** the gates of a ranch.

5. Doing the work or extending the ranch is like the Gospel of the **Kingdom**.

For more of this book or other Garden Publishing Company books use this Order Form.

Name:_____

Address of Buyer:_____

_____

_____

Email:_____   Phone:_____

Desired book: How Many * :

_____   _____

_____

_____

Send this Order Form to the following address, and we will contact you about your order and will be glad to assist you with aquiring our literature:

Garden Publishing Company LLC.
10403 U.S. Highway 87 N.
Sterling City, TX
              76951

*Discounts available on large orders.

For a complete list of our titles, visit us at
www.Gardenpublishingcompany.com

CPSIA information can be obtained
at www.ICGtesting.com
Printed in the USA
LVHW071944300921
698929LV00001BA/13

* 9 7 8 0 9 8 3 3 3 7 7 0 6 *